Gay Heaven Is a Dance Floor but I Can't Relax

charles theonia

ADVANCE PRAISE

"*Gay Heaven Is a Dance Floor but I Can't Relax* gives me the same kind of excitement and imaginative heat that obsessing over the glossy photo middles of queer biographies does. These poems collectively form a watery slide between past and present, care and anxiety, form and formlessness, verb and noun. We can live large in the slippage between the relational and the overwhelmingly mysterious. It would be so easy to fall into a nostalgic hole, but charles isn't that kind of poet. Rather, we dance (or write) into the polymorphous dawn, 'the extended cut, a technology for sensing forever.' I'm grateful to have these poems for how they welcome us in through surreal syntax that then somehow forms a new grammar where metabolic harmony with cats and capybaras, zinnias and rambutans, is the norm, is the gay heaven."

- Stacy Szymaszek

"'Lucky for us we dream in landscapes / beyond our experience,' writes charles theonia in the long poem opening their electric debut collection, and readers are all the luckier for it. Brimming with a sense of the possible, among its many offerings are 'other arrangements of the self'; the dance of bodies (textual and not) entangled in sound; and portals to utopias. It shares Arthur Russell's 'compulsion to keep remaking this world.' This world can't become on its own, hence its gregarious erotics. Jump in!"

- Mónica de la Torre

"Nothing is not gay, and neither space nor time can prevent people from touching in charles theonia's new collection of poems, *Gay Heaven Is a Dance Floor but I Can't Relax*, in which language is motioned to meet desire, to rouse it, spark it, make it public and then make it echo—because why shouldn't it? theonia's poems are for creatures of feeling who want both/and. They arouse, resound and satisfy."

- Shiv Kotecha

"The poems in *Gay Heaven is a Dance Floor but I Can't Relax* possess astonishing depths of love in their arrangements of words and sounds, in their amusement with and within exuberant complexities, and in their utter resistance to giving in to harm and harm's byways. The long title poem, on and for and with Arthur Russell, is a cascade of forms and voices channeled through dance and the untouch into the continuousness of collective knowledge, movement and grief in the face of devastation. And then like Martin Wong, among many other sources of art and hope, charles theonia digs the way firemen smell, listens for sounds waiting for an open mouth, and knows 'Begin can be replaced with any word that brings you closer.' This book is a companion for life."

- Anselm Berrigan

"charles theonia's poems are everything!"

- Tourmaline

Published in the United States by:
Archway Editions, a division of powerHouse Cultural Entertainment, Inc.
32 Adams Street
Brooklyn, NY 11201
e-mail: info@powerHouseBooks.com
website: www.archwayeditions.us

Daniel Power, CEO
Chris Molnar, Editorial Director
Nicodemus Nicoludis, Managing Editor
Naomi Falk, Senior Editor
Caitlin Forst, Contributing Editor

Edited by Nicodemus Nicoludis
Proofread by José Carpio

Library of Congress Control Number: 2023950881

ISBN 978-1-64823-052-3

Printed by Toppan

First edition, 2024

10 9 8 7 6 5 4 3 2 1

Cover image: Joe Brainard, *Untitled (Thirty Squares)*, c. 1973, mixed media on paper, 13 1/2 x 10 1/2 in. Courtesy of the collection of Mark L. Brock and the Estate of Joe Brainard

Printed and bound in China

Gay Heaven Is a Dance Floor but I Can't Relax

charles theonia

Archway Editions, Brooklyn, NY

CONTENTS

EARTHLY REASONS

say what you will about cats, but I don't see
any of you breaking into the bathroom
out of love for me

I really do savor the moment I open the morning
door and liquid cats spill in

a favorite thing about plural cats
is, listening, you have no idea
how many there are

their foreheads' light milk smell

a like-minded person across the world
designed a perfume called Fluffy Brow

I'd like to visit the island
where cats outnumber people

the parallel islands of foxes, rabbits

lucky for us we dream in landscapes
beyond our experience

desert mountains scrolling by

into silver monkey and capybara
hot springs float with steamy oranges

into passion fruit, its pink egg
into two white cups, form
holding itself open

messy hair of the rambutan
its pearly egg into its own glow

blueberry vinegar
a canker sore
brightens the mouth

a walk on the sunny side

into Kelly's 7-hour disco
research playlist

the extended cut, a technology
for sensing forever

Wild Heart dressing room video, 1981

into mallet instruments, when Carly
drops the beat on don't give it UP
when Gerard says my heart
in hiding / stirred for a bird

the bouquet in my lobby said Kayla, I'm an idiot
and an asshole

every year I can hardly believe we live
on a planet where flowers grow on trees

our gay beach nutcracker sociality
communal limearita into pink plastic chalice
the piss fence, rainbows, literal dolphins, all of us
human chain into riptide, vomiting
saltwater back on shore to straddle
each other on hot sand, cheering
when the clouds part back

into octopuses underwater
turning colors in their sleep

their arm brains, visible
thoughts, light
they see with their skin

Hannah says we shouldn't stop
eating octopuses because of how smart
they are but how hard they try to escape

into pleasure of knowing
how something works, revulsion
at how we found out

into our expanses of bleached, silent reefs

I haven't even made it into human pain
I spend my time writing poems
and Wendy says we need those
less than a brick through a window as she
keeps writing them too

if the poem into is all those
who swipe it forward
sit for court support, manage
a bail fund, spark a rent strike
bring meals, share
meds, walk friends home

there's a lot to go looking for

via Agnes' room at Dia I had no reason
to worry it wouldn't be there each
time I returned, by cellphone
photos of the 17th-century still life
lizard reaching their forked tongue
up tulip, via Picard arguing
before a Starfleet tribunal that Data
should be referred to not as it, but he
by June becoming, in front of us, a menace
to her enemies, via Alice always crotch
-naked for music, unowning all seeds
and when Bernadette goes nothing outside

will cure you but everything's outside
when Arthur goes it's a big old world
with nothing in it / I can't wait to see you
another minute

I feel both of that

my external endocrine system
advances in vegan cheese
your ass ascending a staircase
into rain on the shower skylight
I look forward to pickles especially pink
endorphins, of any origin
what we do after the nation and after the police
my hand up your overall shorts and happy
animals running into me

NORMAL GIRLS

I FELL TO THE EARTH MOUTH FIRST

It's bad enough this earth suit
keeps trying to kiss me

I left the bed open and clouds got in

My gut flaps worse if I finger
this feeling heavy with wings

prone to shedding butterfly
scales I willfully mistake for invitations

How on the moon could I expect love

It takes a few days' ugly differences
to decide if hope's embarrassing
or a serial devastation

A new thought can't yet
hold its own weight

Wet and buckling under myself
I turn to painting lip gloss boys

Erections blush across the land

If no works are installed in the far
corner of the gallery
become the work yourself

The red extent of my empty throat
suggests I steal my outline back

I FEEL UGLY EYES CREATING ME

In 1996, they looked up and said, these kids are uglier to us than other ones. Let's wager everyone feels the same

That's the scientific field of sexology

I read about it in a tweet

> University students, masked to group status, judged the physical attractiveness
> of girls with gender identity disorder and clinical and normal control girls,
> whose photographs were taken at the time of assessment (mean age, 6.6 years)

More recently, Anne Carson translated Ibykos' fragment 286, first into English, then into a more limited pool of language: the "wrong words" of other people's texts

The sexologists found that pathologized children were uglier on average to the adults enlisted as aestheticians

They wondered if this had something to do with an objective face

Reading, I said, let's get our friends together and make the sexologists talk with our ugly tongues

Don't get me wrong, I did write a Personals ad ISO the Herakles to my Geryon (pick me up as you get off the bus from hell, and make it hot fast and full of feeling), which yielded one hour of unsatisfying sex and a pen pal in Australia

Not ashamed to say I loved / him for his beauty / As I would again / If he came near

Beauty tempts, doesn't it. It would mean they were wrong about us

On the other hand, Anne Carson hasn't been a reliable friend. For one thing, she has a habit of bringing up Venus Xtravaganza when she has a point to make about men (Gabriel, 2018)

It may be tempting to explain her away as one of us, unrealized, too reluctant to touch the heat of wanting to literally be Oscar Wilde to her cold cheek. I suspect she's more interested in being so unlike other girls that she had to swallow a hot gay ghost and try to stomach him

Her crisis stalls at the evaporating edge of ~female~: before it can burn off, she licks the essentialism from her lips

That's that, and yet it isn't. I like her methods of wrongbeing. I take them back to the social, to citation's study of shared life

These ugly little kids were my contemporaries and as weird-looking as I, or maybe – delightfully – more so

I want to find out how ugly we can grow up to be

TESTOSTERONE SEX FORUM

An old guy did ask some pretty dumb questions.
He hesitates. On people like me. My life + feeling.
Considerably masculine + substantially feminine.
Bath oil, boxing matches, a sense of humor.
Measure my interest in women, girls. My female
trouble is structural. He didn't deny (masculine!)
understanding (feminine!). Pretty, how the hell.
Normal, GOD. Oh, to cry in a bar, objective,
anyone could do. Except I'm not interested
in encouragement. I told him how I can enjoy
my body. The extent to which I cooperate, I'll
be in significantly less understanding. I mean,
I'm bellyward with desire over here. I remind
myself it will all turn out clinical in the end.
The whole spiel. My ablutions are my body and
my body is me. If my Brut deodorant OKs me

BEWARE, A DEADLY FOE IS NEAR

they tell the receiver
you are lovely

no, ugly
thinking of an absent

zinnia, you'll always
I still

tranquilize my
shame, gay life

thee only
do I love

cheerful
bluebell humility

walking on air
false and gay

understanding objectives
fickleness for all

occasions give me
a gladiolus

and I'll girlhood
substantially for you

in secret ivy, the extent
to which I live

but for
fascination

stupidity
grant me one smile

rose leaf you may hope
daisy, I'll never tell

normal
hyacinth

CLINICAL CURIOSITY

Before my wanting to be me on you perks up
lust soaks the improbable space it happens across

I look to you one chair over in the gender clinic
deliquescing with me in the non-profit heat

where unbelievably I've never had a crush
on a single overworked nurse practitioner

even the time they sloshed my own blood all over me
but how have you been in the continual girl fight

I'd lost track and now they're handing me
a cup into which I'll go maneuver my evidentiary piss

Goodbye, I'll be at the beach tomorrow
if you'd like to liquify me there as well

My kingdom for another chance to enter
the weather system of our coverup and sweat

This is why I love waiting rooms
There's still a chance I could get better

WE COULDN'T ENCRUST LIFE WITH LOVE

the body turns out to be a metabolism, a place where questions are fleshy, digested

substance looks restless in your ill-fitting uncool girl machine

while we busy ourselves, trying to girl in fits and starts

there turns out to be something stuck in your procedures

shit takes place, the living weight smeared between your teeth

churning out beauty, too moist, substantial, too real, we didn't know what real was

ugly, on the other hand, does its own thing

intimate, uncomfortable, funny, poised

in your nostril, the condition for making a painting

trying to embarrass the uncertain

extent to which material gropes for form

an open fly, you look down at your creation

and blurt   my god, you're me

GROUP EFFECT

At night I dove for mussels too early for air
and the middle of my hair fell out

SOPHIE asked if you could see it

Sleeping, we entered a local moment
in our suspension pool of collectivizing loss

Someone's crying in the box next to me

The moon I hadn't seen is no longer already full

Sounds she left ring out the shimmering
extent to which we're prettily unreal

There's no need for anyone to hear what we would
sound like if we hadn't intervened

Oh, release me to elselessness. So that's
where we're going

The un-inside,
our best side, resurfacing itself

PINK TRANSMISSION

I felt expired, but like

I was going to eat myself anyway

the snow, in turn, gets wet

with easy caresses

my feeling was backlit

and I couldn't correct for it

clenched at the bottom of a pink pool

the girled know how it got so fucked up

sashay, friends, sashay

public gestures dust glancing fingers

part clouds to nuzzle the slick little moon

draining the secret from the objective, I feel

we do and don't belong to just

ourselves, pooling

at the bottom of a living mouth

IF YOU SQUINT WITH YOUR EARS

Placelessness undoes itself in dust

Distance between you and you may bruise to the degree that we don't give up looking

and an anyhow occurrence offers surface for thought

Put a feeling down and look at it from across the room

The keyboard is a lifeform and we're doing at least a little bit more loving

than they prognosticated for our emotional disorder

You can't become on your own

That's an open inventory of I haven't lost it yet, or I think I know where I left it

Looking for the next pebble forever

At this point I've lived many indoor hours in the restorative company of Beverly Glenn-Copeland

Where he flutters, listening moments propagate:

One thought, brightly colored, attracts others to spread its pollen

It's a feeling I know to be false, that everyone else is outdoors in the sun

If form is forever, it will have to fall apart over and under again

I want to admit the earnestness of this last year in his electronic garden

It makes me feel wide enough to know

everybody is no accident

It's as close to a universal broadcast

just like together is optional — won't you look for it

A SELF PORTRAIT FOR YOU (DOUBLEDICKS)

Reach out and support any one part of your body with any other

When each is at least momentarily an onlooker

wouldn't be able to discern you from you

cuddling up into a constitutive puddle

Ideally we'll each have access to at least two dicks

of various provenance, they can rub enough to generate

a charge or the capacity to interiorize all of us at once

Meanwhile I'm strength training to fit all of yous

I mean mucous strong, like, fucking tensile

between any two outcrops of me until our fucking achieves

a socially constructed dailiness, exquisite and ordinary

and I haven't forgotten how to accommodate the correlational

molecules of you into me, and the eye catches

up with the internal world

On a basic level we like to see

one go in and out of another

We just haven't tired of it yet

and for encapsulation in public space

we watch Björk's dextrous, coterminous tongues

The video forms a membrane over our heads

tilting at the temples, opting out of a body

plan that limits one to one and lit

up from the inside. Gradually

walking by it on my ways home

I realized this bar, which was not

a gay bar, but a bar where we

went to be gay, wouldn't open

back up again, but now

my interior connects to yours

A juice exchange, our renewable materials

I can't keep myself   from collecting new insides

for all yous   in and out   and in again   and in

FOLDED INVENTORY

A-Side

I thought I could use some help, so I read my friends

With some, I've eaten veggie burgers, dim sum

Others were cross-generational communications

I read a chance operator's letters unprepared

to have my feelings hurt. I get protective

of people I've never met. On the other side

I note the absences, what we didn't say

Light is better. You're so much

looser as a wave of light

Turn the painting to the wall and come back

We have worlds

happening between us

But I don't want to deny the rest

B-Side

Before I go on skimming over and under words of others
coming to me down up streams of power and out of order
process pulls itself to the surface, dripping
in gooseflesh and ready for answers

Reading *After Lorca*, I wrote it out:

Life is not noble, sacred, or good
and a cocksucker will always want more of it

While I slept, Rainer and Shiv translated my poems into English

How do the words sound when I'm one the one reading them

I am the least difficult of men. All I want is boundless love

Of course, he said, Spicer couldn't stand O'Hara

but since then they are dead, and the dead are very patient

I keep at it: I wanted Mark Aguhar to pick up the phone

the work was all the objects in her
wavy silk room

her pink spread
precision face

the opening thought

"Girl"
then
"If"

if I say myself through what she said

trans masc is an unsatisfying
category / faggot comes closer

I can't think of another word
so broad, capacious, and unwilling
to let me in

a name does hardly more than nothing if you count in the unit of one
and though a scroll through many pages might gesture to otherwise
it doesn't do much to say you're white in the poem

without porosity, an opening onto what it's read

folding in to meet an earlier
text, other arrangements of the self
paper folds back and rubs one name on another
I turn to *Dear Angel of Death*, to help me read
backwards, to write with others, in the slippery

contact of citation (you might get your sources wet)

every time we read someone, we touch
the papers touching them
the page is where we keep
looking, where we come from

that is to say, I keep trying to read myself into being

thinking in Spicer won't make me an automatic fag
thinking in O'Hara won't make me a lover
lamenting the orchards of my own delectable boredom
rereading White won't make me feel easier to read
I can coat myself in Aguhar's petals, but they won't stick

it's no use being, we just get to read side by side

the textual discontinuous
surfaces touching
up to each other, to offer
relation's aftertouch
an offer to be there in collective
difference and reading
forward again which is after all

PUBLIC FANTASY

TRUTH GAME

OPTIMIST

I think I am an optimist because I see many cats, but 9 out of 10 are plastic bags

SOMETHING WRONG

With enough conviction, and for at least a little while, almost anyone can convince me I've done something wrong

PRIME DIRECTIVE

My prime directive is to not bother anyone. But I keep writing poetry

BLURTING

(I wish I didn't)

DO IT

but I don't know what I want until I'm doing it

BASIC

Reading Judith Butler made me trans

THE TRUTH

And "the truth"—why is the truth so narrow-minded?

I WAS ABOUT TO ORDER AN IMPOSSIBLE BAGEL

When a chihuahua woke me up from a dream of a basketball machine called Sensitive Boy Sensations, 50 cents to play

RESTAURANT

If I were a restaurant, I wouldn't go back to me

COMPANIONSHIP

It would be better to be completely encased

NEED

My therapist said I have a "gaping hole of need"

WHO ASKED YOU?

I like to think I keep my need hole pretty neat along the edges

HEAVENLY BREAKFAST

In a communal situation, bisexuality has to be of at least passing interest to everyone

TODAY

Today is a good day to look at a photo of early Samuel R. Delany

BIG HANDS

That gif of a big hand squeezing juice from a shampoo ginger flower

AFFINITY POLITICS

My enduring affinity for art by gay men who don't care about me

"COMMUNITY"

A lake full of identical jellyfish, looking at itself

CROWD OF THE DAMNED (1197)

I do miss Riis beach all fall, winter, and spring

EROTICS OF THE ABSENT MIND

If my mind is going to be elsewhere, you better believe I'm making the most of the hole it left

WHO ASKED YOU?

As soon as one joke is over, you need another one

MOUTH WEATHER

I wake up unwilling with a dog on my neck, everything moving sluggish molecular cold. The kitchen table is a desk so I don't have to step from the stream of your commentary or the walls heating up in morning's directions. A dog is about bringing the outside in while there is still an outside. Attention alters the temperature: movement on the level of vibration. Slight openings to press a cheek to and express the workday pores. Approach is a sensation. We're heading in non-parallel directions, leaving touch on the table. I invite you into the space of my body, for study. Discovering operations of nearness and the adaptor I need to interface with your inner delight. Everything on the table helps me reach for it. A chihuahua sleeps for eighteen hours a day. I extend our bubble with a tongue and snowfall begins, leaving work obsolete. I like it when you tell me where your mouth has been. Begin can be replaced with any word that brings you closer

LIGHT STUDY IN ONE BREATH

overhead lighting is abusive says our diva Mariah
and when she sings I get kinda hectic inside, don't you
feel expanse and containment lever open the moment
before, groping in its absence, at some point I forgot
the room was still there when I wasn't
underlit by screens, seeing in from street's rosy bricks
to neighbor cat golden in their fish tank, modernist
chandeliers of midwinter, the least day, then it's all
downhill from here until it isn't, we like this shapeless
season, lets us be shapeless too, Trish says that she
is transsexual of course lets them know they are
women and men, one day I'm she in pink earbuds
and sir without, chalcedonies glow on hands
with their own light and what about that private
sensation of purpose walking upblock thrumming
bulbs about to pop street lights flicker and most
everyone wants to be reflected back in sweet
sweet fantasy, the one thing I'm good at

THE PEOPLE'S BEACH

on your leash I'm accounted for
femmes cuddle up on the sand
you grab my ass   say you like
to see us enjoying each other

driveby stench of the water
pollution plant   police copters
agitate overhead   they dragged
a guy naked down the boardwalk
when his towel fell   up beach
private hammocks   palm trees
for rent   vs.   nutcrackers
on our seedier stretch

rosy lizard insides
read sticky   lychee
skin   I'm reading Bob Glück's
gyroscopic   nipples
you're   pursestrung
under pasties   honey
gauze dissolving   stitches

me   I'm years out
and still livid pink

resolution?   I don't know her

we sink in   even the book is sweaty

THE COLOR OF JOY IS PINK

the pink of us is inside and highly specific
community goes on nebulizing outward forever
wouldn't you rather pick an affinity group
or three we'd get into more and better trouble
that way than in the Brooklyn Volunteer
Accountability Corps where the creeps
just walk off regardless into the forever of us
but the more of you the better and every day
you never read the books I like
even when I buy them for you twice
and still the color of us is I bet you
wouldn't unless you knew I was looking

all along the self keeps atomizing and joy
is a shared term I don't know the name for
I'm here for rent parties or to hold your hand
in the hospital where the self of us is more
contested than ever in your unnecessary
untruths when you have everything right here

everything's not enough I know it never is
enough is the color of you me and the rest of it
let's cut your hair plus drink each day a little
more or less and recommit to slipping further
as it happens I'm not doing anything but this

WHAT IS GLITTER

I agreed not to describe   even vaguely
each thrilling although unpretty anything
wasn't for me   but you   liked it   so I did

everyone clicks til we get here
evening's executive functioning   drift
you ask and I do   something sideways of it

anything we do is now called glitter
I don't like everyone but you
know those   inklings   once in awhile

break down mid word   and keep on wording
I'm worried about   tomorrow when it comes
they don't want anyone   to know it's glitter

disposable takes one thousand years to degrade
when the light goes purple   and you whisper   Prince
can I come in?

LET'S GET OUT OF HERE / COIN FLIP

being already late I thought I'd stop
and finish my page it read   not solving
my problems until they occur I
ever suddenly realized you were gone
the calendar said undergo 21 days
of garlic to become a woman
tails   I'm behind because I didn't
know I'd want to be here   heads
distracted by a shadow   heads held
between stations tails   consumed by envy
heads undone by seasonal   shifts in relation
tails waved by pondlight   heads tied up
in public fantasy too far for touch
tails the sun is over   there like during
that time of day plastics   rustle
hairs on my arm   your breath
I know we're not   I moved
everything aside   trying to find it

FOUR TREES A MONTH

it's Abigail's birthday so we chew
her food for her   entrucking
after dinner   the sky's low
with clouds   she says it'll feel
this way   when we don't have
sky at all   just a close expanse
of cover   in our last years
of plants and animals
Bell wants to learn four
trees a month   visitor
from the future overcome
by the sight of a living
horse   we swish zillions
of arcade baskets   shooting
for three in the last ten seconds

when Kelly can't find unflavored
chapstick they say help me
my family's dying   when something
made them gay they say it ruined my life
Sol says one coral can externalize its
stomach to digest another if they get
too close   a line of Bernadette misread
we were supposed to have sex
without knowing anyone

my face on loose   I use it all the same
we don't want to do   what we have
to live   I reach for Midwinter Day
but it's lost in off-season Montauk
sand rolling out in dry ice fog
I sit down to remember lists
art by friends clothing trash   nothing
too small   dreams where one becomes
another gesture   to ways of loving
out of time   a man who can stand in
for her whole past in any dream
and living looks like pulling on
his clothes when he can't leave
the house   I wear Sol's sweatshirt
before they take it back to sleep

MUD LIBRARY

one of my long-gone boyfriends I never met suggests
instead of writing poetry I pick up the telephone

naturally, there are days when everyone I want to call is dead

I present as two ears   listening to each other

hit the library to get all of you on the horn at once

instead of worrying about coming along
so long behind   I would like to propose the comfort
of lying down   sinking
in the rich mud of others

good for the skin   your words sucking into my mouth

in the mud library there are other denizens   we extend
our ears together

it is good to go to the library with friends
you can slide your laptop across the table
to say is this too much   I call Frank O'Hara
my boyfriend and go lie down in the mud

they say   not so far   go on ahead

isn't that what a phone is   wet and distant
sound waiting for an open mouth

SELF-TIMER / YOU PEEK OUT

sleeping hands   hair that rises
I make my preparations
interpreting the   involuntary
body   sticky jacaranda cover
black tea with violets   memory
makes me flush   across
the actual world   I stay
completely still   and lose
my shit   seconds before I
see in the dark

my favorite
letters weren't
addressed to me
that's us   before we got
there   I see Arthur by
the river with his walkman
listening to his own tapes
every day   to get them
right   even the ones
when I'm not by the
river   echo
hum   neither is he

BIG HEAT (MARTIN WONG INDEX)

I really like the way firemen
smell   bricks in the bathtub
boys came in and out
chronically hot   and bothered
you went along   he died on
the other side of the country
everything spells   BO   sweat   smoke
look out on the fire escape
where you're from is less
than social chance occasions
come in   sit down
you're a fireman again   in reality
I'm only into him for the smell
night's big heat   looking in
windows meet me
in a doorway   there are still stars
and silence in the city
downstairs with a rose
I didn't know how much apart
there were no trees
in the streets   gardens
came later   bricks
a portal   over   over
Paco and Cupcake freaked freely
through heaven's hole   almost

sealed off   in my Lower East Side
the street screen flashes Ed Koch
waking up every morning to say
Well   we're still in New York!
I wake up every morning to say   Well
structural malice still kills!
but what does that do
for you   your giddy fireman
costume   your up against
not in   knew there's no
belonging   no reason
not to come closer

ARE YOU HEARING IT NOW

after movement   rejoining the still
breath catches   in the particulars
little snores mean   you haven't
died in your sleep   rain that
touches everything   yes now
on shore we praise the iconic
intro of dance with somebody
east river cruise boat party   our ears
autofilled   it was girls just wanna have
fun on the rocks   cops hassle
girls with beer cans   we watch
til they move on   something's
swelling   warning in the water
someone too close   looking too much
whatever that sounds like
my pulse with it   I don't hear
with bluebells my   peripherals
but other sounds that   probably
not or probably   shoulder me
on the train   mutter why ya
standing there faggot   instead
of screaming worldlessly   or whipping
out your dick   our sleeping shoulders
but if it were   or would that
if instead when I get to   what are we

willing to give up if we   gets
bigger for real   the real Whitney
key change lifts me up to meet it
soughing   little frogs   purring
wind shivers   fur brushing fur
it's ok   it's ok   it's ok

CLEAR WEATHER

going outside doesn't
glisten   I don't want
to be good   nor love

                          he said careful   we
                                  don't like that here
                          and that   on your block

losing   control my hand
your pocket slipping   follow
cloud coat   upstreet via

                  my dream of Cedar   outside
                      the Associated   is that you!
                              it was   and we hugged

algae in another season   she
jumped   were a lawn   green
dog   not mine to wash

                          living nine years at her size
                          how could you do it   or
                      at most   alternatively not

are raccoons growing rounder
infinitesimal   tonight while
a lot in it   you wait for me pondside

          early   magnolia fur
          set in articulated snow
     claw nor love   control my hand

upstreet via cloud cover   shifting
when I   cover you   kumquat
comes off   leaving on foot   for green

          bloom algae   in another
     sky purples obscurely   happy
     for having   nowhere to be

tap to hear space
inside its
indefinite vision

     in our night   is night forever
          up to   waking up
     leaving   on foot at one

LILY PAD

before I went too far and added violet

at the last minute without exchanging

a word we forgot to break the rules

I could have popped the bottle when

Mona said champagne on the road is better

absorbed I dream you're mad at me waiting

above a pond we fuck on the soft air

expectation is a narrative error

marking the hours by how often you empty

the rain bucket is better than work

it is recommended that we reserve

dream reenactment for the third date

or later walk in the belly between our

apartments full of news I kiss you against

a public wall to trade the morning for

warm winter sun prosecco a tricky secret

with each new person arises an ever

more highly specified self-consciousness

I would like to believe you don't mind

I reset skin distance at each beginning

could go on forever as the morning had

extended itself down a pink hallway

we met without sending our thoughts ahead

OPEN HOURS

Given a finitude of dances
I'd like as many you can give me
Exhausted in the glad spent morning
from work in afternoon means time
for breakfast and arriving back at you
with the inside of me
In hours as material as these
love's both concentric selfishness,
no time to love everyone even
if we'd like, and since you pointed to
the rabbit in the moon I've had
a new relationship to fullness

There are so many of us, oh good
but morning is a recurrent slip
from I forgo it. The hours
go on exchanging somewhere
for elsewhere in love's index
I'm ready when you are
in the next place we go looking

BIOLOGICAL SEX ON THE BEACH

on the earth's edge, there's a red streak where red used to be

the sky is down to earth

it wants to give up distinction and let the world in

and the world spreadeagles beneath it, foreshortened

by pleasure, or some other totalizing experience

but pleasure gets my bet, why not

bet on a fantasy of daily life, when life

like the sun, has been hard to get ahold of

yes, perhaps you guessed it, I'm dreaming

of another gritty day at the gay beach:

waves lap, seafoam trembles, condoms surf

and asses, thank goodness, jiggle

our mascara (figurative) is running (literal)

turning the sand a radiant mauve beneath us

mini planes trespass overhead, artificial clouds

spell out BIOLOGICAL SEX ON THE BEACH

hell yeah we grew these belly hairs and tits ourselves

we're drinking margarita slushies and forming a dream

pop band, we're called Biological Sex on the Beach

the crabs looking to get a pinch are just off screen

we're being legislated against as we sip

and we wrote our own blurbs, how do you do:

we're "unintelligible" or "intelligible" on alternating petals

how could the sky be so flat, wouldn't it like to come in

that's not my handwriting but it is my message

GAY HEAVEN IS A DANCE FLOOR BUT I CAN'T RELAX

our mouths go and find you there

make dense spaces   kiss

so brief   come from in and looking

out we   alternate us   across songs

dance makes time plastic   reach all nights

in one and home at dawn   subdivided

smaller cells   the week   sun fingers brushing

smell   salt   dust   poppers   kissing

friends i want to see   stall in circles

lost hours expand   i'm always time

slipped   during dance

untouch across the room   I go

standing in where I am   right now

hear all disco years at once   that's you

and me   in through the ear

rewinding tape   me and   you

that's once   at years   disco all

hear but   thighs between our

thighs   come with us

Bring enough tapes to last your time out of the house. At the intersection of avant garde cellist and disco hitmaker, there lived Arthur Russell. Every day, he walked to the Hudson River, listening to his echoes. He died of AIDS-related causes in 1992. In found space, dance leaves time residue. AIDS is not over. You can still feel every assshaking in the slippery air. Arthur didn't want you to come in and play his drum line. He wanted you to bring yourself into him bringing you together in his oceanic room. That's where i came looking. i was in my bedroom arranging discos. He was on the Staten Island Ferry, editing cassette tapes in his head. i was at Hey Queen, losing my nostalgia for the nightlife. He had his eyes closed on the Gallery dance floor. i heard transmissions, sweat. Light flecks

Landlords shut off the heat in apartments of tenants with AIDS

i can't remember where i read this

They turned the city over at market rate

Everything we do gets in on history

Now: a figment

Utopia: a compulsion to keep remaking this world

i see him in accounts, where he was and wasn't:

       – I came back to find the landlord had beaten holes
       in the wall and bricks were lying in my bed

       – When someone collapsed, we called Man down
       The guards wouldn't come in without a hazmat suit

       – The president required several years before he could bring
       himself to note the existence of the disease

       – The hospital wouldn't take him

       – We sat in hospice shifts

       – In the morning they would come in and retrieve the body

I go   what about
standing   the Hudson
in where I am   standing
right now   to meet you

I was intrigued by some guy on the telephone. Arthur's name was Charles
then it wasn't. He was in the Gem Spa buying an ice cream

My name wasn't charles, then it was

Accept a fragmentation of a person

We moved around it in different directions

Secrets he didn't have

That was how we met

Writing a diary

Thinking of how to write songs that say thank you

Or what's gonna happen

our sounds go

        and find you there

      make correspondence   sticky

brief

              i'm always

                   ear slipped

              for chance

         all nights once

        thighs rewind

        the room to you

He looked "weird" when he danced, but that didn't bother him.
He was imagining what the disco was like. A packet of scented
dust he kept in his pocket

i look weird when i dance, but that doesn't stop me. i could
dissolve in a mass of sweat and breath. Mesh, blue lipstick
Latex, sequins. All my friends at once

The words are never in the place you would expect them to be

His question was what made them get out into the sticky. What pulled them apart into sound

i overheard a sense of being here, fell on my face lovedancing, feeling for my glasses along the collective

You could pick the needle up anywhere and put it down, and it always sounds the same. His question was what's with this kid standing against the wall untouching everyone

i look weird because i'm imagining what being then, being sure sounds like. Extendable structure. Dipped in and out of at will

The children of the Gallery were in no doubt that this was fabulous

spilled beer yeast pull

dusty salt reconstitutes

hair flip   fingers net

light flecks   skin

lick   flecks spin

if I can't

go and find   you there

one night in all

rewinding
                        dawn

His question was an account of our bodies entangled in sound

Partygoers gave themselves up to a heady cocktail of collective motion

If he were alive today he'd be going dancing later

Approaching the haptic libidinal build

He was definitely a white-boy dancer

Cut-up and reaching for a collaborative mix

Or sitting against the wall smiling

Watching everyone give it all

A proposal for an incorporative form

The way people speak music through the dance floor

The hospitals insisted on gloves and a medical mask

Elastic around the ears

Untouch across the room

Are you wondering how long it will be

It was hard to go out to a disco and start dancing

The way medicine was going, his faltering voice

People were living in hope and public force

When the eerily empty dance floor became too much to bear

He seemed so real to me it was like, that's not gonna happen

If we're alive then, we'll see ourselves historicized early

The club shut its doors in the spring of 1988, the year i was born

His question was how we learn to see our atmospheric preconditions

In 2019, Gilead prices Truvada at $21,000 a year

An HIV-positive prisoner gets a felony charge for spitting on a deputy jailer

An art pop star throws a PrEP-themed dance party

What is I doing here

Who would i know if i opened my mouth. Questions

because i don't know how to answer them

i go standing in where i am right now

now I'm heading
to nothing
cause it's no more fun
going down
through the Pines

what I'm doing
I did before
and that's all
I see driving

where you were
i'm more gone
outside you now
making friends
i forget

to find you
untouch
too in it
anyone was

driving sixteen miles
I'm looking
for something
I don't want
to do

and I wonder
at all where I
would be
if I can't go
and find
you there

there looking
away when we talk
the pattern of
our bed in the sky
the quiet week

flips over
fell off the path
lying in the reeds
sand spills
each step i meet

If he were alive today, i could have met him by now. If you want

to reach my world it's full of pleasure. His question

was afterlife transmission, ongoingness of the disco

PrEP4ALL activists dig up evidence of Gilead's public

patent violations. The CDC maintains that HIV

cannot be transmitted through saliva

PILLS COST PENNIES / GREED COSTS LIVES

Your whole body's got to lose

HIV IS NOT A CRIME / CRIMINALIZING IT IS

Every sense and notion before you [inaudible at 2:36]

 IF I DIE OF AIDS—FORGET BURIAL—

JUST DROP MY BODY ON THE STEPS OF THE F.D.A.

By morning, papers under-reported us

Get on up and do it again

It had to happen; I was going to meet him because I kept going back. When interviewing Arthur Russell, think fishy, and if you don't think fishy, think wet. He loved the sound of rewinding tape, and I learned to love that sound too. World of Echo didn't address AIDS explicitly. Oceanic formlessness. Casio keyboards on sailboats. In the gentle undersea rhythms of a coral reef, the Blue Tang displays his dreamy colouration. I would carry his cello

i'm looking across the room where we would be

This song "I'll Be Your Friend" has been on for 15 or more minutes

You're in the disco keeping up your correspondence

So I decided to try and finish a letter to you

The crowd is pleasantly mixed

One really forlorn good looking big guy is walking around with a cane

Here he comes again (!)

Men move me aside by the waist

Menergy. . . we all know the feelin'

One guy was walking around with a pillow on his chest

i feel a compulsion to remake the world

i'm in my bedroom remixing poem and disco, spilling a sticky beer

i'm in your archives, reading a dermatological appointment confirmation

Letters from friends returning your tapes from desk piles and footwells

I think of you with Walkman headphones on

Bringing your letter home at dawn and never sending it

Could you call me next Sunday (collect)

our masses pull apart

reconstitute mouths

across salt I wondered

years

divided

where to find you and how

songs touch across the room

ove
I feel lo
o
o

i   goes
slipping in

gay life: you want to dance

then you look around and see who you could be dancing with

I thought at the disco

if i were alive then, i'd be in the library looking back

your smile across the open dance floor

my hands up your sweater, from the beginning

it was always better not to think

as anyone who has gone

to find you there can tell you

disco understands itself

maybe you spilled onto me

i leave half-connected

i feel the ongoingness

i keep going back

I want to share this love in heaven on

the night flips over

and on, and on, and on rewinds

everytime we kiss

there's more of it

we confirm the new world meeting us

everytime a song comes on

hey that's our song

AFTERWARD   (HEADY COLLECTIVE)

[Utopia: a compulsion to keep remaking this world]

> *Wild Combination: A Portrait of Arthur Russell.*
> Directed by Matt Wolf, 2008

[That was how we met]

> "Q+A: Tom Lee on His Life with and
> without Arthur Russell." *The Fader*, 2008

[Casio keyboards on sailboats]

> Frank Owen, "Echo Beach," Interview with
> Arthur Russell for *Melody Maker*, 1987

[One guy was walking around with a pillow on his chest]

> Letters from the Arthur Russell archives
> at the New York Public Library

[The children of the Gallery were in no doubt that this was fabulous]

> Tim Lawrence. *Hold On to Your Dreams: Arthur Russell
> and the Downtown Music Scene, 1973-1992*, 2009

[If they were alive today, they would still be living with AIDS]

Fierce Pussy, "Get Up Everybody and Sing," 2010

[We sat in hospice shifts]

My notes from Brian Carmichael's reading at "Caring Break (inside and) Out," for *What Would an HIV Doula Do?*, 2019

[The ongoingness / the entangled / history]

"How We Do Illness: Twenty-One Questions to Consider When Embarking on AIDS-Related Cultural Production." *Triple Canopy*, 2018. A conversation facilitated by Corrine Fitzpatrick and Ted Kerr

[Are you wondering how long it will be]

Stop AIDS or Else leaflet, 1989 (distributed to the occupants of cars stopped on the Golden Gate Bridge)

[he was definitely a white-boy dancer]

Stuart Aitken, "Disco Savant." *Wax Poetics*, 2007

[feeling for my glasses along the collective]

"Metropolitan," a painting by Louis Fratino, 2019

[haptic, libidinal]

Ricardo Montez, *Keith Haring's Line: Race and the Performance of Desire*, 2020

[I thought at the disco]

Douglas Crimp, "DISSS-CO (A Fragment)," 2008

[disco understands itself]

Tan Lin, "Disco as Operating System, Part 1," 2008

[PILLS COST PENNIES / GREED COSTS LIVES]

Signs from protests against HIV-criminalization and pharmaceutical price-gouging, 2012 and 2019

[I want to see all my friends at once]

Dinosaur L, "Go Bang," 1981

[JUST DROP MY BODY ON THE STEPS OF THE F.D.A.]

David Wojnarowicz's jacket, 1988

[Your whole body's got to lose]

Suzy Q, "Get On Up and Do It Again," 1981

[Lovedancing]

Loose Joints, "Is It All Over My Face," 1980

[Every time we kiss]

Essex Hemphill, "American Wedding," 1992

[I feel love]

Donna Summer, "I Feel Love" (15-minute
Patrick Cowley mix), 1982

[I want to share this love in heaven / on and on]

Sylvester, "Be with You," 1982

[We all know the feelin']

Patrick Cowley, "Menergy," 1981

[I go standing in where I am right now]

Arthur Russell, "Losing My Taste for the Nightlife."
Recorded over the '80s, released posthumously in 1994

NOTES (LIGHTWAVES):

Along with the sources noted in "Heady Collective," these poems incorporate, reconstitute, and refer to language from other texts:

"Earthly Reasons"
Tweets by Wendy Trevino and Hannah Black, June Jordan's "I Must Become a Menace to My Enemies," Alice Notley's *Benediction*, Bernadette Mayer's "The Way to Keep Going in Antarctica," Arthur Russell's "That's Us / Wild Combination," Gerard Manley Hopkins' "The Windhover," and "Carly Rae Jepsen's "Now That I Found You"

"I Fell to the Earth Mouth First"
T Clutch Fleischmann's *Syzygy, Beauty* and a dream of instructions for a S*an D. Henry-Smith gallery install

"I Feel Ugly Eyes Creating Me"
Kay Gabriel's "Specters of Dying Empire: The Case of Carson's Bacchae," Anne Carson's "Possessive Used as a Drink (Me)" and *The Beauty of the Husband*, and "Physical attractiveness of girls with gender identity disorder" by S. R. Fridell , K. J. Zucker, et al.

"Testosterone Sex Forum"
Lou Sullivan's diaries, *We Both Laughed in Pleasure*

"Beware, a Deadly Foe is Near"
Databases of the Victorian language of flowers

"Group Effect"
SOPHIE's *Oil of Every Pearl's Un-Insides*

"Clinical Curiosity"
    Trish Salah's *Lyric Sexology*

"We Couldn't Encrust Life with Love"
    Amy Sillman's "Shit Happens: Notes on Awkwardness"

"Pink Transmission"
    Oki Sogumi's "Beautiful Fighting Girl"

"A Self Portrait for You"
    A photograph of the same title by Elle Pérez.

"If You Squint with Your Ears"
    An interview with (and the lyrics of) Beverly Glenn-Copeland

"Folded Inventory"
    Agnes Martin's *Writings*, Mark Aguhar's Tumblr *Call Out Queen*, Simone White's *Dear Angel of Death*, and Jack Spicer's *The Holy Grail* and *After Lorca*, and Frank O'Hara's "Meditations in an Emergency" and "Joe's Jacket"

"Truth Game"
    This poem takes the form of Joe Brainard's mini essays, a line from his "Wednesday July 7th, 1971 (A Greyhound Bus Trip)," and another from Samuel R. Delany's *Heavenly Breakfast*

"Mouth Weather"
    Renee Gladman's *Calamities*

"(Light Study in One Breath)"
    Mariah Carey's "Fantasy" and Trish Salah's "Interlude 1: Out of Time"

"The People's Beach"
    Robert Glück's *Jack the Modernist*

"The Color of Joy Is Pink"
    A tweet by Diana Ross

"What Is Glitter"
    Caity Weaver's investigative glitter journalism

"Let's Get Out of Here / Coin Flip"
    A letter from John Cage to Merce Cunningham

"Four Trees a Month"
    Frank O'Hara's "Joe's Jacket" and Bernadette Mayer's "Midwinter Day"

"Mud Library"
    Frank O'Hara's "Personism: A Manifesto"

"Self-Timer / You Peek Out"
    Arthur Russell's "That's Us / Wild Combination" again

"Big Heat"
    Titles and text from the paintings and sculptures of Martin Wong and "The Glory That Was
    Wrong: El 'Chino Malo' Approximates Nuyorico" by Roy Pérez

"Lily Pad"
    Agnès Varda's *Vagabond* and a dream of Rainer Diana Hamilton's

"Biological Sex on the Beach"
    A painting of the same name by Eli Hill and the blurb Arthur Russell wrote for his own record,
    World of Echo: "UNINTELLIGIBLE"

ACKNOWLEDGMENTS

Some of these poems previously appeared, often in earlier forms or under other titles, in Archway Editions' *Journal, Baest*, Black Mountain College Museum's Radio Art Program, *Black Warrior Review, The Brooklyn Rail, Feelings, Guts Magazine, Oversound*, The Poetry Project's *House Party*, Small Press Traffic's *Traffic Report, Social Text, Tagvverk, The Texas Review, Triangle House Review, Women & Performance*, and *We Want It All: An Anthology of Radical Trans Poetics*. Thank you to the editors and to the Foundation for Contemporary Arts for their support.

Thanks to Cat Fitzpatrick, Rainer Diana Hamilton, Shiv Kotecha, Sol Brager, Stacy Szymaszek, Ted Kerr, and Zefyr Lisowski (and all those who found themselves in classes or the short-lived but juicy Juice Exchange with me) for talking to me about these poems.

Particular thanks for good words and times to everyone who offered them at Brooklyn College. My enduring appreciations to Anselm Berrigan, Ben Lerner, Julie Agoos, and Mónica de la Torre.

Over the years of this book's writing, many of those above and Abigail Lloyd, Ali Howell, Anastasia Usinowicz, Bell Kauffmann, Kelly Xio, Kiik An Yuh, Lou Cornum, Marissa Zappas, Maysam Taher, and ray ferreira hung out with me when (which is always) it mattered most.

To Jonah Rosenberg and Shaina Yang for our collaborations around poems in this project, and Francis Weiss Rabkin for long-ago discussions on the subtleties of Queer vs. Gay Heaven (you'll have seen which side of the clouds I set down on).

And to all those who work on preserving and sharing Arthur Russell's work, with particular gratitude to Tom Lee, Steve Knutson and Audika Records, and Doran Walot and the NYPL.

To @martybast and the other guardians of wildlife in Prospect Park.

And everyone else who is has been and will be in my echo collective.

Thank you to Nicodemus Nicoludis and Archway Editions for making this a book, and thanks to Ron Padgett and the estate of Joe Brainard for the cover painting, one of the images that gives me the most delight in a lifetime of delight.

MORE FROM ARCHWAY EDITIONS

Archways 1
(edited by Chris Molnar and Nicodemus Nicoludis)
Archways 2
(edited by Chris Molnar, Nicodemus Nicoludis, and Naomi Falk)
Blake Butler – *Molly*
cokemachineglow: Writing Around Music 2005-2015
(edited by Clayton Purdom)
Claire Donato – *Kind Mirrors, Ugly Ghosts*
Gabriel Kruis – *Acid Virga*
Brantly Martin – *Highway B: Horrorfest*
NDA: An Autofiction Anthology
(edited by Caitlin Forst)
Alice Notley – *Runes and Chords*
Ishmael Reed – *Life Among the Aryans*
Ishmael Reed – *The Haunting of Lin-Manuel Miranda*
Mike Sacks – *Randy & Stinker Lets Loose*
Paul Schrader – *First Reformed*
Stacy Szymaszek – *Famous Hermits*
Erin Taylor – *Bimboland*
charles theonia – *Gay Heaven is a Dance Floor but I Can't Relax*
Unpublishable
(edited by Chris Molnar and Etan Nechin)

FORTHCOMING AUTUMN 2024

John Farris – *Last Poems*
Jasmine Johnson – *Infinite Potential*
Ishmael Reed – *The Conductor*

Archway Editions can be found at your local bookstore or ordered
directly through Simon & Schuster

QUESTIONS? COMMENTS? CONCERNS? SEND CORRESPONDENCE TO:

Archway Editions
c/o powerHouse Books
220 36th St., Building #2
Brooklyn, NY 11232

Archway's mission is to publish the finest authors, at all stages of their careers, who write material which is at odds with the prevailing status quo, both legendary and emerging. This series is designed to be a literary complement to the trailblazing artbooks of powerHouse Books proper, pocket-sized texts that are guaranteed to alter the way you see the world.

Our imprint is genre-blind with a goal to publish unconventional books for the widest possible audience.

Power to indie print.